EVERYBODY IS AFRAID OF SOMETHING, BUT THESE FEARS HAVE NAMES.

A is for
Arachnophobia:
A fear of spiders

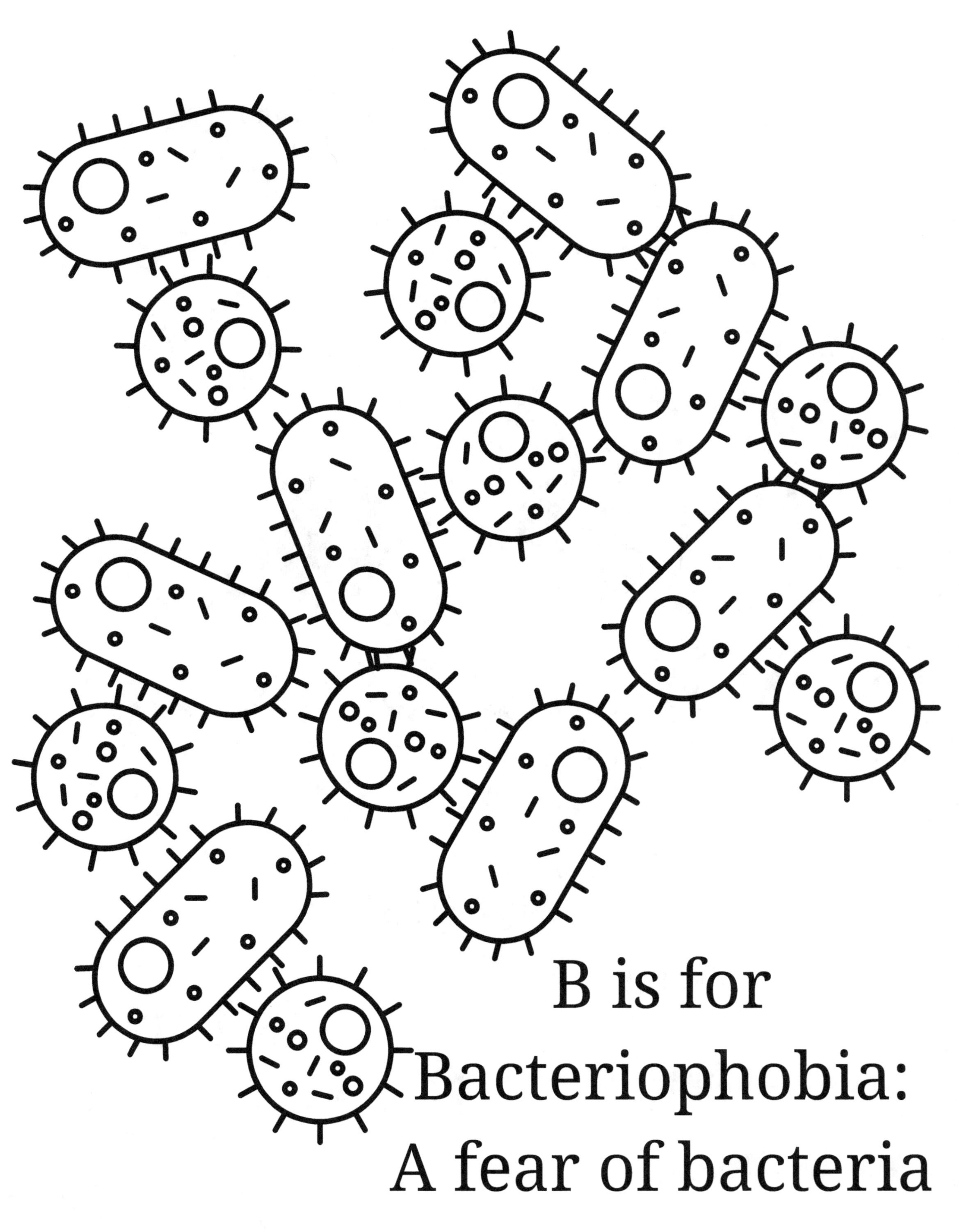
B is for
Bacteriophobia:
A fear of bacteria

C is for
Coulrophobia:
A fear of clowns

D is for
Dendrophobia:
A fear of trees

E is for
Ecophobia:
A fear of the home

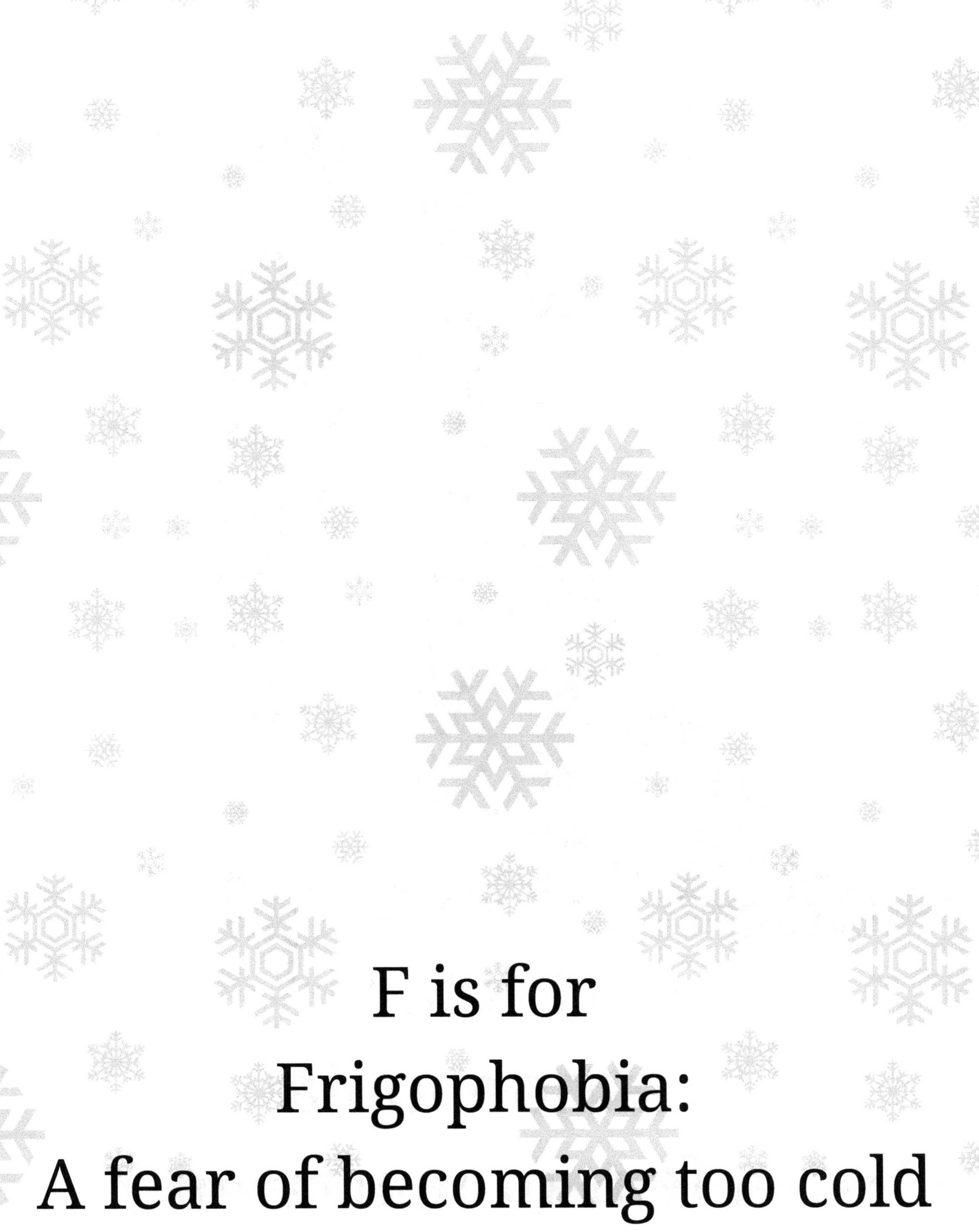

F is for
Frigophobia:
A fear of becoming too cold

G is for
Gamophobia:
A fear of marriage

H is for
Heliophobia:
A fear of the sun

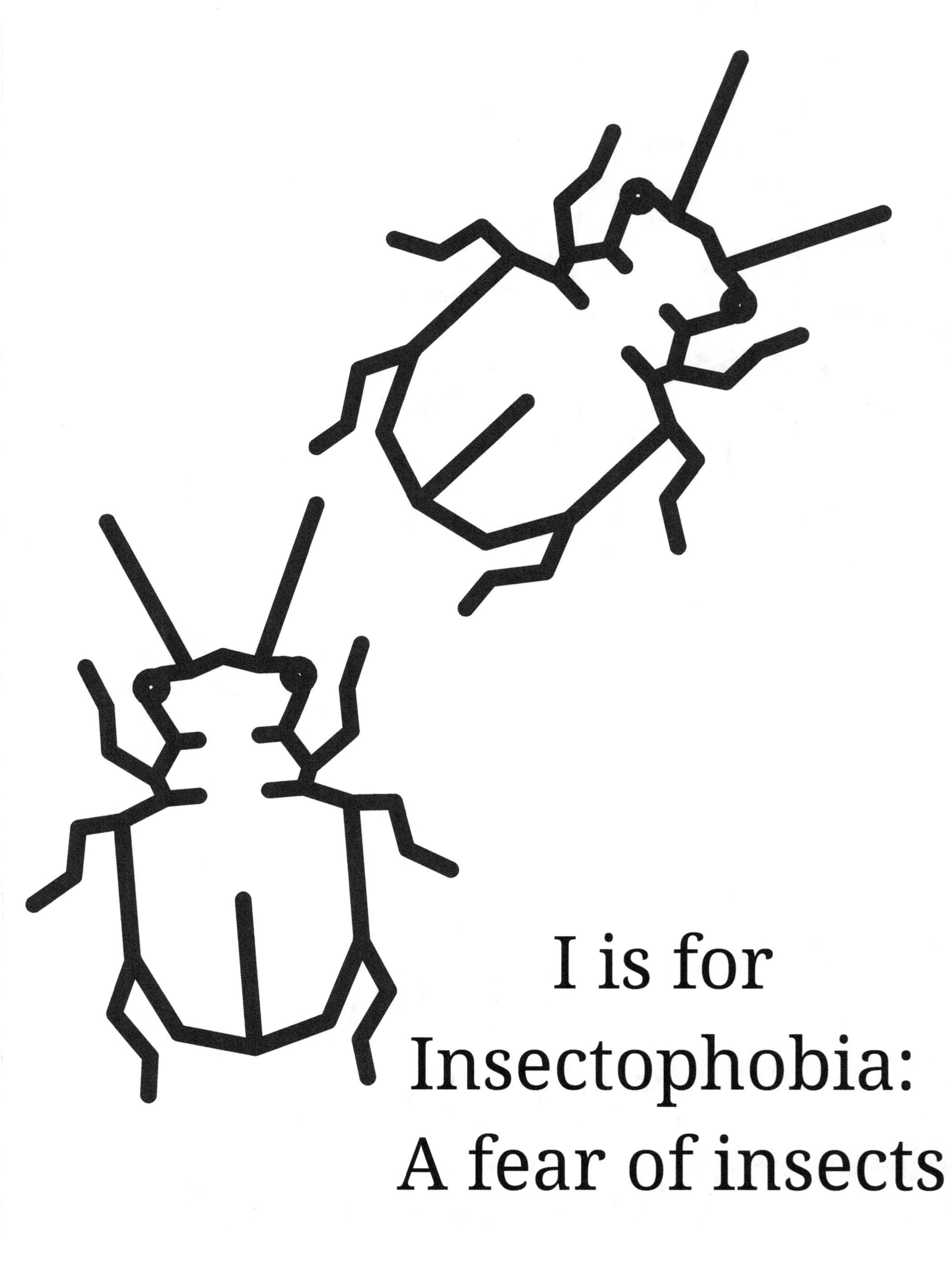

I is for
Insectophobia:
A fear of insects

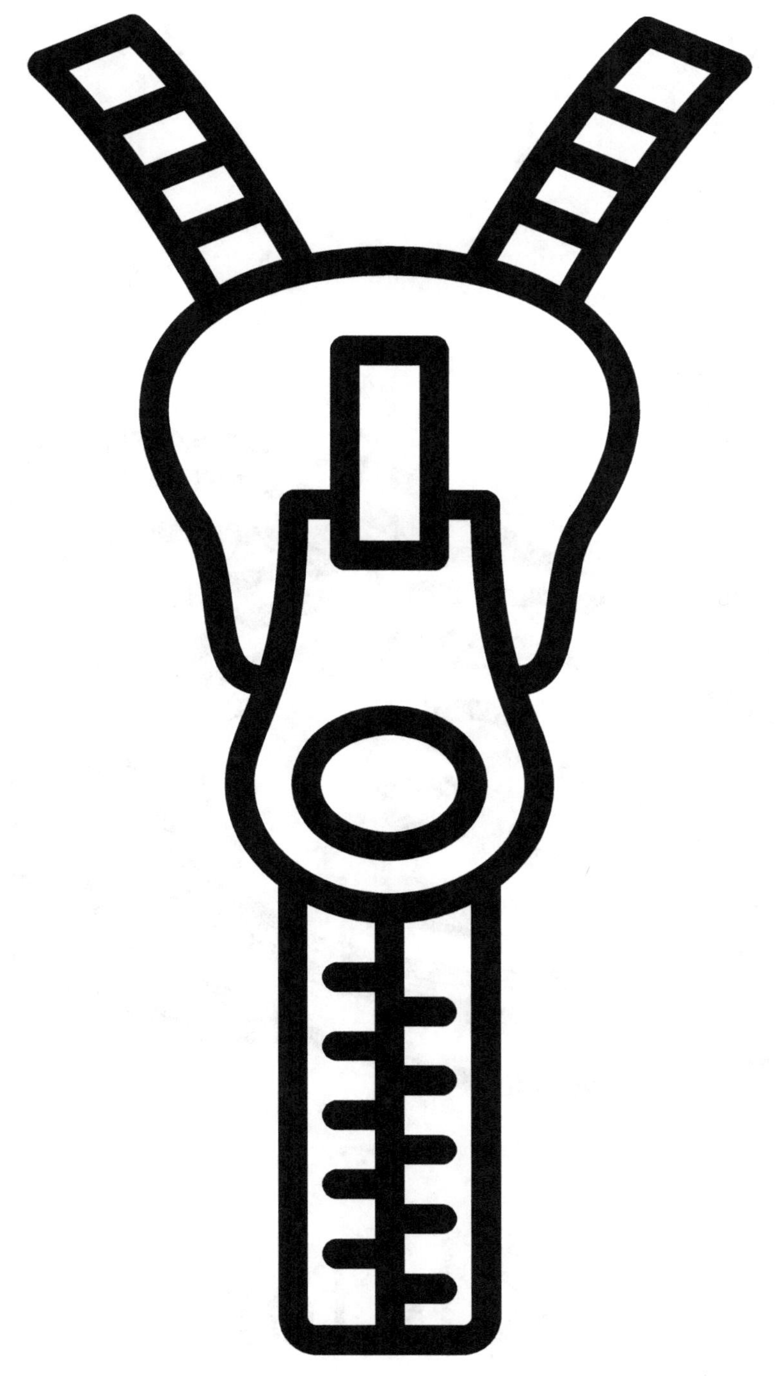

J is for
Jumaphobia:
A fear of zippers

K is for
Koumpounophobia:
A fear of buttons

L is for
Leukophobia:
A fear of the color white

M is for
Mageirocophobia:
A fear of cooking

N is for

Necrophobia:

A fear of death

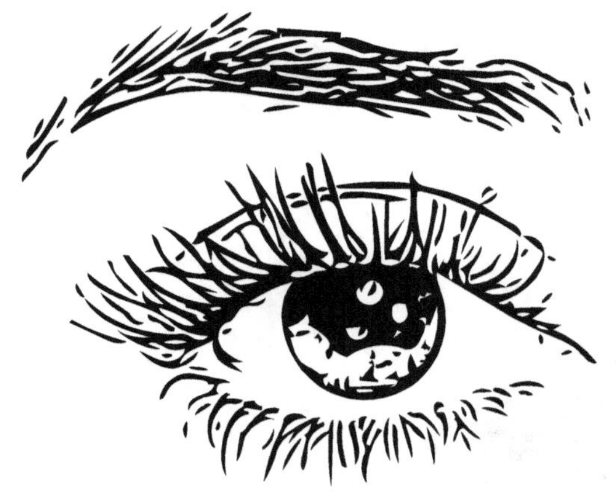
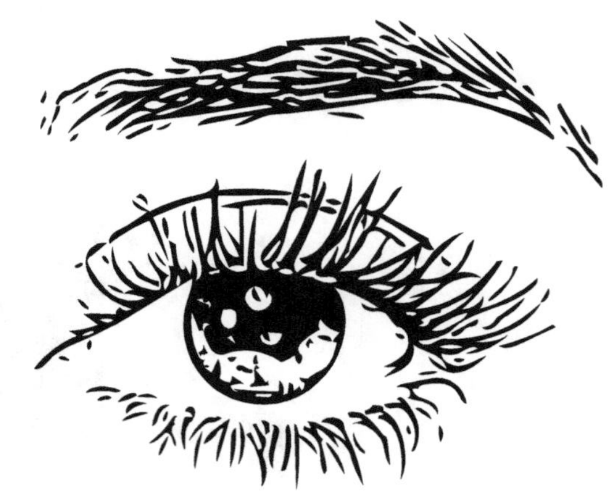

O is for Ommetaphobia: A fear of eyes

P is for
Pyrophobia:
A fear of fire

Q is for
Quadriplegiphobia:
A fear of quadriplegics

R is for
Robophobia:
A fear of robots

S is for
Spectrophobia:
A fear of mirrors

T is for
Triskaidekaphobia:
A fear of the number thirteen

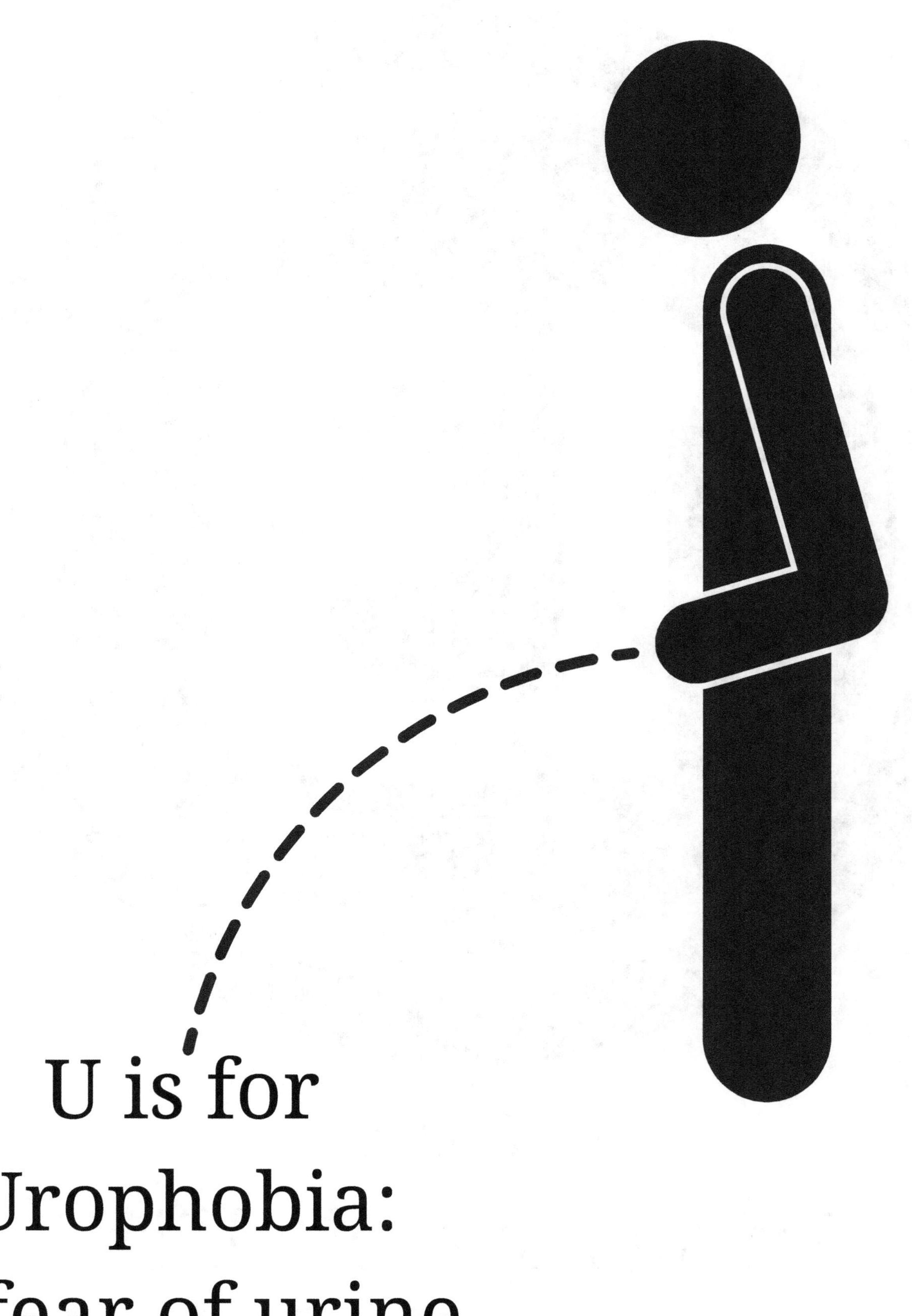

U is for
Urophobia:
A fear of urine

V is for
Vehophobia:
A fear of driving

W is for
Wiccaphobia:
A fear of witchcraft

X is for
Xyrophobia:
A fear of razors

Y is for
Ymophobia:
A fear of being contrary

Z is for Zoophobia: A fear of animals

www.ingramcontent.com/pod-product-compliance
Lightning Source LLC
LaVergne TN
LVHW080600160826
845677LV00010B/1931

* 9 7 9 8 3 5 6 6 5 1 5 9 5 *